COLD WAR

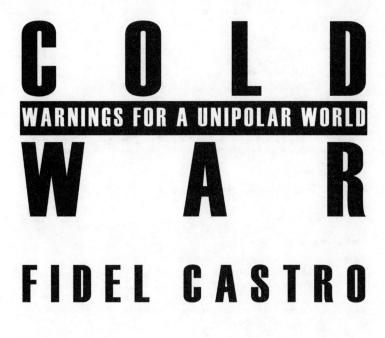

COLD WAR

WARNINGS FOR A UNIPOLAR WORLD

FIDEL CASTRO

PUBLISHED IN ASSOCIATION WITH THE OFFICE OF PUBLICATIONS,

CUBAN COUNCIL OF STATE

Ocean Press
Melbourne ■ New York
www.oceanbooks.com.au

Cover design by Sean Walsh

ISBN 1-876175-77-X

Library of Congress Catalog Card No: 2003107190

First Printed in Australia 2003

Published by Ocean Press

Australia: GPO Box 3279, Melbourne, Victoria 3001, Australia
Fax: (61-3) 9329 5040 Tel: (61-3) 9326 4280
E-mail: info@oceanbooks.com.au

USA: PO Box 1186, Old Chelsea Stn., New York, NY 10113-1186, USA
Tel: (718) 246-4160

Ocean Press Distributors:

United States and Canada: **Consortium Book Sales and Distribution**
Tel: 1-800-283-3572   www.cbsd.com

Australia and New Zealand: **Palgrave Macmillan**
E-mail: customer.service@macmillan.com.au

Britain and Europe: **Pluto Books**
E-mail: pluto@plutobooks.com

Cuba and Latin America: **Ocean Press**
E-mail: oceanhav@enet.cu

ocean

www.oceanbooks.com.au
info@oceanbooks.com.au

AN INTERVIEW FOR THE CNN/BBC SERIES

"THE COLD WAR"

WITH

DR. FIDEL CASTRO RUZ

PRESIDENT OF THE REPUBLIC OF CUBA

MARCH 19, 1998

CNN — *Mr. President, we will be talking about the role played by Cuba during the Cold War, concentrating on the period and the events that occurred between 1954 and 1990. I propose that we begin in 1954, when the government of Jacobo Arbenz was overthrown in Guatemala. To what extent did this event affect your political thinking at that time?*

FIDEL CASTRO — At that moment, I was isolated in a prison cell at the Isle of Pines penitentiary, as a result of the attack on [Cuban dictator Fulgencio] Batista's Moncada military fortress on July 26, 1953. So, by then, I had come a long way in my political and revolutionary thinking.

What happened in Guatemala did not really come as a surprise to me, but it did very much anger us and it proved to us the impossibility of making profound social changes in the absence of a deep revolution.

President Arbenz and his group in the country's leadership were a team of progressive people who wanted to work for the Guatemalan people — for the most part very poor, indigenous people — and, actually, the basic measure they had taken was land reform.

I was not able to get to know his politics in any depth, but I know that what triggered the action against Jacobo Arbenz in

Guatemala was the Land Reform Act. Immediately afterwards, the U.S. Government, through the Central Intelligence Agency (CIA), developed a plan to overthrow Arbenz. They tried a similar coup later in Cuba with the Bay of Pigs invasion, in 1961.

They mobilized and trained a number of men, on the Honduran border I think, and I also think they launched the main attack on Guatemala from Honduras with several planes and the complicity of some sectors of the military.

The people supported Arbenz but they were unarmed; there was no way they could fight, and the military, of course, was unwilling to hand weapons over to the people. That is why the attack succeeded and, in a matter of days, the Arbenz government was removed from power.

That made a deep impression on all the progressive forces of the hemisphere and on Latin American public opinion, because it was perceived as an interventionist action and a violation of the Guatemalan people's sovereignty. A government that had wanted to work for the people had been overthrown.

Some of our comrades who had taken part in the Moncada and Bayamo actions on July 26, 1953, were in Guatemala at the time. Che was also there; his name was Ernesto Guevara but as he was Argentine the others called him "Che." I think he was working as a doctor there, and these events had a great impact on him; he was in fact traumatized by what happened.

Later, our small group of four or five comrades, including Che, moved to Mexico. I met Che in Mexico and from my talks with him I remember he was terribly angry and embittered about those events that had interrupted a relatively simple change that was not even radical — a fair and necessary land reform for that country.

As for us, it reaffirmed the conviction that the making of a revolution requires the support of the people, and an armed people; in the conditions of our hemisphere, a revolution also required a new army.

At the time, our perspective was focused not so much on Latin America, but on our own country, since our experiences derived from what we had known in Cuba and what we had lived through in Cuba. We had already reached certain conclusions and certain concepts, but they were fundamentally related to Cuba. What we had in mind then was not the revolution in Latin America but in Cuba.

We were certainly concerned about Latin America. We were familiar with the history of the independence struggles in this hemisphere, with [Simón] Bolívar's ideas and his dreams of a union of Latin American countries at a time when neither means of communication nor transport were what they are today. And although he conceived of a united Latin America at a time when that was practically impossible, he was, nonetheless, a great visionary and a harbinger of those ideas.

At the time we also had thoughts of a united Latin America. Ever since we were students — in the years 1946 and 1947 — we had been active supporters of specific Latin American causes. For example, one of my first activities at university was as a member of a committee for Puerto Rican independence. I had not yet studied Marxism, but an essentially nationalist and Latin American sentiment led me to support Albizu Campos in his struggle for the independence of Puerto Rico. We supported the Panamanians in their claims for the recovery of the [Panama] Canal. We supported the Argentines in their demands over the Malvinas [the Falkland Islands]. We were opposed to the continued existence of European colonies in this hemisphere at that time — Jamaica and the vast majority of Caribbean countries were not independent. Furthermore, we supported the revolutionary movement in the Dominican Republic against [dictator Rafael] Trujillo and, in general, the struggles of students against repressive and bloody governments like the one I just mentioned, or like Somoza's in Nicaragua or other countries. But we still were not thinking of a radical revolution in Latin America; we were thinking about Cuba and our revolutionary ideas.

Of course, the lesson we learned from that experience [in Guatemala] was further proof of U.S. interventionist policy and our countries' lack of independence as well as of how hard our struggle would be after all.

When did you realize, Mr. President, that carrying through the ideals of the Cuban Revolution might mean taking sides in the Cold War?

Well, actually, we did not take sides in the Cold War, nor was the Cold War our creation. We wanted to make a revolution in Cuba, a deep and radical revolution. We were by then thinking of a socialist revolution, but in the more distant future.

At the time, in 1952, we had to face up to a situation where Batista's military coup d'état, carried out several weeks before elections were to have been held, had destroyed the constitutional legal system. That coup removed every possibility for legal and peaceful struggle, although I must confess that by then it was clear to me that for a revolution in Cuba to produce really deep changes it had to be preceded by a revolutionary struggle for power.

We were already thinking this through in 1952. We had reached such a conclusion, but we could still operate within an institutional framework. We had in mind a clear and advanced program, but the coup d'état removed any possibility of peaceful action.

In summary, we had already reached the conclusion that the revolution had to be achieved by gaining and holding political power and power had to be taken in a revolutionary manner because the capitalist system and society was designed to last indefinitely, and the constitutional and legal mechanisms had become an obstacle for the eventual realization of a truly deep revolution.

The coup d'état changed our whole strategy. We had first thought of fighting together with all the other forces to bring the country back to constitutional rule, but the hard and bitter reality was that the other political forces were incapable of uniting and undertaking serious plans. We were then forced to use our movement, which had grown rapidly in a short period of time — hardly a year after the coup we had over 1,000 people organized and trained in the open, not clandestinely, in a sort of independent revolutionary action. We worked with teams of people who were practically unknown in political circles; thus, we were able to conduct our work not in a clandestine way but in almost normal conditions.

That situation did not change until our [July 26, 1953] attack on the Moncada Barracks in Oriente, which marked the beginning of the struggle. Before the coup on March 10, 1952, we had even been hoping for the support of certain sectors of the military. We had been denouncing the injustices committed against the soldiers, that is, we were not just defending the workers, peasants, students and the most disadvantaged sections of the population, but also the soldiers who were forced to work the farms owned by key politicians and senior military bosses. We had been carrying forward a campaign to undermine discipline within the armed forces by denouncing the abuses and injustices committed against the soldiers. In other words, our program also included the possibility of winning the soldiers' support. With the coup d'état, however, we were forced to fight the army directly, to fight against the soldiers.

This brought about a serious conflict because Batista had been firmly established among the soldiers from the days he had carried out his first coup on September 4, 1933, backed by a sergeants' movement. He had won great influence in the army by handing out a lot of privileges and promoting sergeants to lieutenants, captains, colonels and generals. In this way he had gained great authority.

The constitutional governments which followed in 1944 did nothing to change that situation within the army, so, eight years later, the army remained the same and Batista retained a great deal of influence within it. [In 1933] it was easy for Batista to displace a constitutional government completely discredited by corruption; after the March 10 coup, however, we had to confront a regime that had the support of its troops. So, putting aside the idea that a revolution could be made with or without the army but never against the army, we [nevertheless] made the unflinching decision to organize a revolutionary struggle against the army, something no one would have believed possible based on the vast differences between the regime's forces and our own.

We were not thinking of the Cold War because we had a hot war here in our country, against a repressive, brutal and reactionary regime. Our concentration was on Cuba, not on the Cold War. We believed in the possibility of achieving our aims and, in fact, the revolution triumphed.

It triumphed with the total support of the people and with a new army forged in the struggle. It wasn't as in Guatemala where the government implementing land reform had an old, professional army and an unarmed people. At the end of the war the total number of men we had with arms was 3,000. But with the full support of the people we overthrew an army, police and navy totaling 80,000 men; we took their weapons and created a new people's army, with peasants, workers and students — people of very modest means. Those were certainly the conditions required to make a revolution and defend it. That's why, and there's no need for further explanations, the plan in Guatemala was successful while the later Bay of Pigs invasion failed, despite the fact it had been inspired by that earlier experience of dirty war and using mercenary forces to carry it through.

That was no time for us to think about the Cold War.

Besides, we were somewhat naive: we believed that there really was a certain international order, that certain international principles really existed and that the sovereignty of our country would be respected. Not much time had passed since World War II and it seemed that a certain respect had been created in the world's conscience for the sovereignty of nations. So, as we had the people's support and enough forces to defend the revolution, as well as a just government program in favor of the people, we believed that our country's sovereignty would be respected.

I think we deceived ourselves. Actually, despite experiences such as that of Arbenz in Guatemala, we believed that the age of direct intervention was definitely over. Because we considered our cause to be just and because we were working for the people, with the support and sympathy of international public opinion and even the support of many U.S. citizens, we believed that our country would be respected.

By then, we certainly had a very advanced program called the Moncada Program. I won't describe it but it included quite a radical land reform and an equally radical urban reform. It also included the punishment of war criminals — that is, the trial and sentencing of those who had committed major crimes. Unfortunately, many escaped and went to the United States. The worst criminals, or many of the worst, left on January 1, 1959, for the United States, with all the money they had stolen and with the heavy burden of thousands of murders on their consciences. That is the whole and irritating truth of what happened in our country at the triumph of the revolution.

But [in Cuba] laws had been previously adopted and the trials were unlike those of Nuremberg because at Nuremberg there were trials without prior laws and against a principle of law, recognized from the Roman era, whereby punishment could not be applied without legal precedent.

We had a certain amount of legal training, so as the war proceeded we had been adopting laws in the liberated territories regarding war criminals, and they were therefore judged in compliance with corresponding legal procedure. We said to the people, let there be no revenge, justice will be done, and we succeeded in not having a single example of revenge exacted by the population.

When the revolution triumphed it was an example of order: there was no pillaging or crime; no one was dragged through the streets as had occurred in other places; there were no assassinations; there was perfect order and sentences were passed according to law and in courts of justice. But the people demanded punishment for the crimes, and it did not occur here as in other countries like Argentina where the principle of due obedience of orders was invoked. [A key principle governing war crimes trials is that obedience to the orders of a superior is no defense.]

Punishment of war criminals had been unheard of in the history of Latin America and that is why there are now situations where, even in countries like Spain, investigations are being made into Chilean and Argentine members of the military and they are being put on trial for crimes committed many thousands of miles away, and in foreign territory. In the history of Latin America and also of Cuba, there have been many bloody regimes and many crimes have been committed, that were never punished. For this reason it was one of the people's demands.

Another demand was the recovery of all embezzled goods; an action undertaken in the first years. There was also severe unemployment. The revolution promised the people jobs and administrative honesty, something that had never truly existed in our country. It promised health programs, which had never existed, and education programs, which did not exist or were very poor, in a country where less than 20 percent of the population really knew how to read and write.

All those social programs and the promise of investing the country's resources in its industrialization were received by the people with great satisfaction, as they were part of the program we intended to carry out at the triumph of the revolution. It wasn't a socialist program at that time, although we were already thinking like socialists and dreaming that, in the future, our country might advance toward socialism. But it was the hostility we encountered and the acts of aggression against our country that accelerated the revolutionary process and led the country to socialism in an accelerated fashion. That is the historical truth. As I said, we felt we had the right to do these things, and the right to be respected, but life has proven how very wrong we were.

I therefore say that we did not involve ourselves in the Cold War but that it was the Cold War that became involved in the Cuban Revolution. It was the United States or the U.S. Administration that brought the Cold War to Cuba.

When the revolution triumphed, we had no relations with the Soviet Union. There was no Soviet ambassador here and we had no trade with the Soviet Union, although we did think our country should trade with every other country in the world and that it should have access to all markets. But we had no relations with the Soviet Union and neither did the Soviet Union have anything to do with the Cuban Revolution.

The socialist character of the revolution was proclaimed on April 16, 1961, almost 30 months after the triumph of the revolution, at the funeral of victims from the bombing of Ciudad Libertad air base conducted by U.S. planes bearing Cuban insignia — an attack similar to that of Pearl Harbor, aimed at destroying the few planes we had prior to the Bay of Pigs invasion. Ciudad Libertad was attacked at dawn on April 15 and at the funeral, in the presence of tens of thousands of armed militia members, socialism was proclaimed. As the dangers and the risks of aggression to our country emerged, we delivered weapons to the people and did not hesitate to purchase weapons and mobilize thousands of citizens.

We did not, however, purchase our first weapons from the socialist bloc, since we did not want to provide a pretext whereby a ship arriving in Cuba with socialist weapons could become a justification for acts of aggression against Cuba. We bought the first weapons from Belgium and Italy — some tens of thousands of automatic rifles in Belgium, and some cannon in Italy. Do you know what happened? Since these countries were very much influenced by the United States, and the U.S. invasion plans were already being prepared, the Italians sent us only the ammunition and some of the cannon we had bought, but not everything. The Belgians sent two or three shipments of arms, the last of which [*La Coubre*] had been sabotaged at its departure point and blew up at the pier in Cuba when hundreds of Cuban workers were unloading it. There were two explosions: the first killed many workers and soldiers, but the second explosion occurred when even more people had gone to help the injured.

The ship had been sabotaged abroad. That story will be known one day. I don't know what documents the CIA may have with information about this or when they might be released.

Look, do you know when the plans to overthrow the revolutionary government began? Hardly six months had passed after the triumph of the revolution, following the enactment of the Agrarian Reform Act. The fight against Cuba began because of land reform. A U.S. law was passed in the month of May [1959] basically unleashing the fight against Cuba, and thus we were brought into the Cold War.

When we could not obtain weapons anywhere else and had no markets for our sugar — they began by limiting our sugar quotas in the United States — when we could no longer buy many things, it was then we decided to purchase weapons from the socialist bloc and that is how the first weapons from the socialist bloc came to Cuba. Just a few months before the Bay of Pigs invasion we received important arms shipments.

We had the weapons we'd taken from Batista, some tens of thousands of weapons we bought in Belgium, and then some hundreds of thousands of rifles we bought in the socialist bloc, because the people had to be armed in order to defend the revolution. That's how we found ourselves involved in what was later called the Cold War. But it can also be said that we did everything possible to avoid getting involved in that Cold War.

Mr. President, moving to the topic of the Missile Crisis, commonly known here in Cuba as the October Crisis. How was the proposal made to you about the missiles and why did you accept them?

The Bay of Pigs invasion had already taken place in April 1961 and it had been defeated; it was an overwhelming defeat attained in less than 72 hours. It is an indisputable fact that the U.S. Administration never accepted that defeat. Although the invasion had not actually been Kennedy's responsibility, since it was a legacy he inherited from the previous administration and those programs and plans were made before Kennedy's inauguration as president in 1961, it fell upon him to endure that defeat. He was honest and brave when he said that victory has many fathers but defeat is an orphan. He took full responsibility but he didn't resign himself to the results and so plans of a different nature, also aimed at destroying the revolution, including the idea to use the U.S. Armed Forces, were immediately set in motion.

We had suspected that such a thing could happen and continued to prepare ourselves, drawing on the experience accumulated in our own war, so that we would be able to resist a U.S. invasion with all the means at our disposal and wage the kind of war suited to that situation.

The year 1962 began and a meeting between Kennedy and Khrushchev took place in Vienna, I don't remember the exact date. Based on those conversations, Nikita reached the conclusion that the U.S. Administration had plans or intentions to carry out an attack against Cuba. He formed that conclusion. I believe one of his arguments was that in the conversations

Kennedy had brought up the example of the [1956] Soviet intervention in Hungary, and Khrushchev interpreted this as a prob-
ing or a kind of warning that a similar thing could happen in
Cuba. Further, a son-in-law of Khrushchev, editor of the news-
paper *Izvestia* — Adzhubei was his name — had visited the
United States and met with U.S. leaders. I think he met Kennedy
as well, and different subjects had been discussed in such a
way, including the situation in Cuba, that Khrushchev's son-
in-law perceived the same intention to attack Cuba.

The Soviets reported this information to us. Of course, by
then we were also very suspicious of the United States, having
lived through the Bay of Pigs invasion and the dirty war before
the Bay of Pigs: dozens and dozens of arms infiltrations and air
drops of weapons, most of which we had been able to seize.
Throughout the dirty war irregular groups managed to operate
in every province of the country, even in the province of Havana.
But we confronted them with an armed people. At the time of
the Bay of Pigs invasion some such groups still remained in the
Escambray Mountains [in central Cuba] but, a few weeks before,
we had mobilized 40,000 soldiers to the area and had reduced
the numbers in those groups from over 1,000 to less than 150.
We paid all the necessary attention to the struggle and succeeded
in neutralizing them.

We had suffered sabotage, pirate attacks, all kinds of aggressions, and not only were we irritated but we were also very
suspicious of the United States, so that the information provided
by the Soviets came as no surprise. Nor did it alarm or worry us
a great deal, because we considered ourselves capable of
resisting aggression.

You might say we were a Vietnam before Vietnam. We knew our territory very well — our mountains — and we had fought in extremely disadvantageous conditions. We had great support in the mountains, on the plains, in the countryside and in the cities, everywhere, and the people were ready to fight. It is historically proven that a country which is willing to fight cannot be defeated. There are many examples, experiences the United States has had, like that of Vietnam. The Soviets have also had such experiences. They had the experience of Afghanistan, for example, although that is a larger, more mountainous country. All the big powers have had such experiences. France had the experience of Algeria, despite the support the French Army received there from a large number of French settlers. Many experiences in modern times have demonstrated that a small country can defend itself against a great power by using adequate tactics and methods of struggle, and we were confident that we could resist.

The Soviet Government's hypothesis (maybe they knew more but they told us only what I have repeated to you), which was the result of the Khrushchev-Kennedy conversations in Vienna and those of the *Izvestia* editor's visit in the United States, had indicated something we very much suspected and very much had in mind.

Now, on May 29, 1962, two emissaries sent by Khrushchev arrived in Havana. One of them was Rashidov, then first secretary of the Communist Party of the Soviet Union in Uzbekistan — the country that now votes against Cuba in the United Nations, making three votes in favor of the [U.S.] blockade — and the other was the head of the Soviet Missile Forces, Biryuzov, a smart and alert marshal. We met — it was a short meeting — and they explained their concerns about an eventual U.S. direct aggression and they asked me what I thought could be done to prevent or avoid such an invasion.

At the time I was far from thinking about missiles and I said: Look, the only way to prevent direct aggression by the United States is to let it be understood that an invasion of Cuba would mean war with the Soviet Union.

The United States has done the same with many countries to which it has given guarantees. It has said: "I am a guarantor for this country and it may not be touched because we would take it as an aggression toward the United States." The United States has applied this principle to many countries of the world.

I felt that a clear and categorical Soviet declaration in such terms could have enough influence and exert enough pressure to prevent a direct invasion. Then they asked me another question, they said: "Yes, but what can be done? How can it be shown that, in fact, an invasion of Cuba would lead to war with the Soviet Union?" It was at this point when they raised the matter of the missiles. They spoke of deploying 42 mid-range missiles in our country and a number of antiaircraft rockets, aircraft and ground forces, as well as a number of Soviet mechanized regiments.

I immediately grasped the situation, realizing they had two concerns: on the one hand, a real concern over an invasion of Cuba, to which they had a great moral obligation from the moment they began buying our sugar, supplying us with weapons and fuel, and supporting us at the United Nations. They had made very strong statements following the Bay of Pigs invasion.

A great atmosphere of sympathy and admiration for Cuba had been growing in the Soviet people because our revolution had emerged on its own, spontaneously, at the doorstep of the United States, something they had never imagined or ever would have believed possible. It had excited an emotional state in the Soviet people, the Soviet leaders and particularly in Khrushchev because Khrushchev believed in his ideas, his doctrines and unquestionably he believed in socialism; so for them, the rise of a revolution in this hemisphere was like a miracle. They were under a great moral obligation to Cuba before their country's public opinion and before world opinion. So, on the one hand, they were truly worried that an invasion might take place but, on the other, I felt, understood, or interpreted at the same time that they also had a strategic interest. The strategic importance of having those missiles in Cuba could be easily perceived.

At that time, also secretly, the United States had moved similar missiles to Turkey and Italy, not very far from Soviet territory. In the case of Turkey, it had been done as secretly as the sending of the mid-range missiles to Cuba.

So, we were faced with a dilemma. We didn't like the idea of having either Soviet missiles or troops here, since it could adversely affect the image of the Cuban Revolution and because by then, with the experience we had gained, we were thinking about revolution in the rest of Latin America. If, when we attacked the Moncada or when we were in prison or fighting in the Sierra Maestra mountains, we had contemplated the struggle against the tyrannical governments of this hemisphere, we had by that time come to the conclusion that truly far-reaching changes could not be made anywhere in Latin America without a far-reaching revolution, that is, without a revolution similar to that which had taken place in Cuba.

We had come to this conclusion and attached great importance to the revolution in Latin America and, of course, a strong Soviet military presence here in the Caribbean was going to deprive the Cuban Revolution of a lot of influence. To the rest of the world, we would simply become a Soviet base.

We were so worried about this that we didn't find the guarantee the missiles could give us particularly appealing, but we looked at things again and analyzed them from another important angle and found an ethical question posed. I thought: If we expect the Soviets to fight for us and take risks for us, and even go to war for us, it would be immoral and cowardly for us to refuse to accept here the presence of missiles which would improve the balance of power for the socialist bloc and the Soviet Union's strategic position. That's how we felt, analyzing it from an ethical viewpoint.

Just as I'm telling you now, I meditated over it in those minutes while they were making their proposal, but I did not and could not give them an answer. I had, however, come to the conclusion that it was our duty to accept the political risk posed by the missiles, bearing in mind we were not so much concerned over either the physical risk or any crisis that could emerge. They could only protect us from an invasion that utilized conventional weapons and we ourselves felt capable of fighting against such an aggression. On the other hand, if for whatever reason nuclear warfare began anywhere in the world, we would be sacrificed.

There was still the matter of our image in Latin America and

they talked with such certainty about the dangers or the possibilities of an invasion of Cuba, could it have been because they already knew some things, had seen some of these secret Pentagon and U.S. Government documents — which have only recently been published — in which the U.S. military had been instructed to fabricate a pretext for an invasion of Cuba?

This has all been published, it is no longer a secret. Many things that were secret at that time are not secret any more. The U.S. Senate has investigated CIA plans to assassinate me, for example, and there were many more such plans besides those discovered by the Senate Committee. These are now uncontested truths; all those plans are now public. The CIA recently published an extensive and very interesting report covering the Bay of Pigs invasion. After 37 years, those truths have been admitted officially. Recently, some historically interesting Pentagon papers were published, on the instructions received by that institution to fabricate an incident justifying an invasion of Cuba. And I wonder: Wouldn't it be possible that a Soviet spy, or a Soviet informant, had told the Soviets of the instructions received by the U.S. military? They never said so to us, but after we have learned all that has been officially published, I have been wondering whether they actually had such information and were not basing their arguments solely on Khrushchev's and Adzhubei's conversations with Kennedy and other officials. They probably knew this but did not say a single word to us because they were very careful, very cautious — and rightly so — with everything related to information obtained through espionage. In any respect, today it is clear that Nikita was right and that an invasion against Cuba was in the making. That is the historical truth. I have not discussed this issue with anybody since the [recent] release of those documents. This is the first time. But those documents show Nikita was right in his theory that an invasion would be launched.

That was how the issue of the missiles was discussed and approved. Later, a long story followed, but that is not relevant now.

You spoke about the [global] balance of power and the way you understood it at that time.

Yes.

Did you feel disappointed with the Soviet attitude at that time?

When?

Did you feel disappointed with respect to the balance of power at that time?

No, because we had not discussed that.

To be able to talk about the global balance of power, we would have needed details that only the Soviets had, such as how many nuclear weapons they had and how many missiles. At the time I thought they had more, since they had been the first to launch a satellite and the first to conquer outer space. I thought in that period they would have made more progress in the development and production of such weapons, but that was something they only achieved later.

There is no doubt that, at that moment, the presence of those missiles in close proximity to the United States meant an improvement in the balance of power, an improvement in their strategic situation, regardless the number of missiles they had, because these could reach their targets sooner. The warning systems for the intercontinental strategic missiles gave more time [to respond], 30 to 35 minutes, while some missiles here, similar to those the United States had in Turkey, gave much less warning time — just eight, 10 or 12 minutes. Do you see it now? Anyone could see that from a military perspective that meant an improvement in their strategic situation.

That is what I could analyze at the time, when I had no other details. Later, with all the research [into the Missile Crisis] — including the research of the McNamara group and the discussions among former members of the Soviet and U.S. military and ourselves — I was able to learn, very recently, that at the time the Soviets had a relatively small number of missiles.

This again reaffirms my belief that the presence of those missiles here at that particular moment was extremely important for the Soviet Union, whom we considered to be our ally, which was supporting us and we expected would fight for us if we were invaded.

Mr. President, were those missiles fully equipped to be fired?

That issue is still being debated but, according to what I was told in a meeting I had on October 26, 1962, with the head of the Soviet military command — who presented a report on the status of his forces — they were all ready.

He said: "Aviation regiment, ready. Ground-to-air rocketry regiment, ready. Mechanized-troops regiments, ready. Tactical nuclear weapons regiment — they had such a regiment — ready. Missile unit, ready." In that report, all the forces were pronounced ready. There have been debates since then and there are different theories, different ideas.

At that moment, the crisis was in full swing and U.S. planes were making low-altitude flights over our targets, something we opposed. That evening I informed the Soviet military command that we would no longer allow low-altitude flights over our territory because they put us at great disadvantage, being that they could launch attacks and destroy the bases. I said so categorically.

We had mobilized all our antiaircraft artillery to protect the missile bases, the strategic missiles and the ground-to-air rockets. They only had one piece with two cannon to defend the ground-to-air rockets, which were only effective after 1,000 meters. That is, their antiaircraft artillery was not exactly the most modern and the U.S. planes were flying at 100 or 200 meters altitude.

We already had hundreds and hundreds of antiaircraft artillery pieces ready, operated by Cubans, so we made the decision on our own, to deploy them around the bases and missiles. We told the Soviets they had made a mistake in letting those planes fly; that it was inconceivable in a war situation where their forces could be destroyed by a surprise air strike.

Moreover, I advised the Soviet chief — I took the liberty to advise him although he was an old and experienced general from World War II — that in the situation in which we found ourselves, in danger of an attack, the strategic missiles should not all be placed on the launching-ramps, that a missile reserve should be kept separately so that if some missiles were destroyed in an air raid, the rest would still be preserved. That was my concrete advice to the Soviet chief.

I remember having later discussed this subject once with [former CIA deputy director] Vernon Walters, an American with links in top circles of the U.S. Administration, and he related his theory that some of the Soviet nuclear warheads were not operational. The Soviet report at the time was that every strategic missile was ready and so were the tactical nuclear missiles. Now, I would not be able to make such an outright statement that not even a screw was missing. All I can tell you is what I knew and how I came to know it, at that moment.

I had contact with the Soviet local command, with whom we made very serious assessments of the situation and the weaponry. I told the Soviet chief that the following day, October 27, our antiaircraft artillery would begin firing against the low-altitude flights. I met with this man on October 26 and said that beginning at dawn on October 27 we would use our antiaircraft weapons.

Mr. President, on October 26 or 27, you wrote a letter to Nikita Khrushchev warning him of the dangers of a U.S. invasion of Cuba. Khrushchev took it that you were urging him to consider a first strike use of nuclear weapons. Were you?

There is some truth in that; there is some truth, but it has never been correctly explained. The exceptional circumstances in which I expressed that idea have never been adequately described.

The letter you are talking about does exist. I do not know if it has been published, but I have it. It is the most passionate letter in history. I had met the Soviet military chief and told him that we would open fire with our antiaircraft artillery and that we could not tolerate low-altitude flights over our territory. We had mobilized all the artillery, taken every measure and observed the situation properly, including the risks of a surprise air strike — troops were being stationed in Florida and other places. I was aware of the complexity of the problem, resulting, among other things, from the very poor and incorrect handling by Khrushchev, and the crisis which placed Kennedy in a very embarrassing, unbearable situation. Because the Soviets' approach had been different from ours, in the months preceding the crisis, I felt there was still something left for me to do.

For a better understanding of what I am explaining, I should say that we had been in favor of releasing to the public the military agreement that had been signed [between Cuba and the Soviet Union], but the Soviets had objected.

From our point of view, what we were doing [in positioning the weapons] was both legally and morally correct, unobjectionable and in full compliance with the principles of international law. We were [also] doing exactly what the United States was doing everywhere else throughout the world: in Asia, Japan, Spain, England and in every country where it had military bases, troops, missiles and strategic bombers, everything.

I said: What we are doing is absolutely legal and we should do it openly, in the eyes of public opinion, and we should say what we are doing and publish this document.

Also, at the end of August [1962], we had sent Che [Guevara] and comrade Emilio Aragonés to meet Khrushchev and give him my message, which was the final draft of the agreement. The first draft they had sent was so poorly drafted and so inappropriate that it was unacceptable — a shoddy piece of political work — so I myself rewrote the draft military agreement, in my own handwriting, because not even typists took part in this. I have it here. Do you want to see it?

Is that it?

Yes, this is it, a facsimile of the final agreement in my own handwriting as I sent it to him. The agreement had been approved de facto; a document had been signed by Raúl [Castro] and Malinovsky between July 2 and 8, and the measures were being implemented but it was not yet publicly known that there was a military pact between the Soviet Union and Cuba.

We were in favor of operating in the public light and not as if something illegal were being done; we wanted to keep all the moral strength of one who is acting within the norms of international law.

I have only mentioned this as an example of the terrible way in which Khrushchev handled the whole period that preceded the crisis, and the crisis itself; this man talking to you here is grateful to Khrushchev and even remembers him with fondness and warmth for all the things he did for us and for the affection and admiration he felt for this little country. But the Soviets made many mistakes, military mistakes of every kind, including some related to the ground-to-air rockets and other things I have already mentioned.

Then, after we had done everything humanly possible, I asked myself: What is still left for me to do? I thought to myself: there is still something and that is to give Khrushchev some encouragement, to prevent him from becoming disheartened.

I was aware of his deep concern for peace. He had a great love for everything he was doing in his country, for his country's development, for all his country's economic plans. He was representing a people that had suffered through a terrible war which cost them over 20 million lives. I knew the Soviets as peace-loving people. I knew the history of World War II very well: the Germans' surprise attack on June 22 [1941], against troops that were not mobilized, against garrisons whose officers were on leave, etc., and I was worried that at such a difficult moment Nikita might hesitate. I was afraid he might waver, that he might make a mistake, and so I said to myself: Well, this is the only thing left for me to do.

I felt things were extremely difficult, in truth because Kennedy made very good use of Khrushchev's mistakes, one such mistake being to get involved in the argument about whether the weapons were offensive or non-offensive.

A pistol is an offensive weapon if I bring it to shoot you. What is an offensive weapon and what weapon is defensive? Offensive weapons were associated in everybody's mind with strategic weapons. When Kennedy talked of offensive weapons, he was thinking about that type of weapon and when Khrushchev talked about it, he was thinking that the objectives of using a weapon defined whether they were defensive or offensive. Those were the criteria from which one and the other set out. But Dobrynin spoke several times with Kennedy and Kennedy's most trusted men and he assured them that there were no offensive weapons, that there was nothing, even when it was impossible to ignore the claims by Kennedy.

Actually, the Soviet leader resorted to deception and, in any political dispute or any dispute for that matter, deception is negative and fruitless. It demoralizes the one who lies, the one who deceives. Worst of all, Kennedy had believed word for word what Khrushchev had told him and he was reacting to all the pressures in his country on the basis of the assurances he had received from the Soviet Government.

In the meantime, we were discussing with our allies our disagreement on this point. In every statement at the United Nations, and everywhere, we said: "We do not have to give any account of the kind of weapons we have. We maintain our right to use those weapons we consider suitable and necessary to defend our country and we need not give anyone an account on that." That was our position. We did not join in the arguments about offensive or non-offensive weapons, the game Khrushchev got trapped in.

I was afraid that [the Soviets] would make a mistake. As I am telling you, I could see the situation was difficult, there was no way out for Kennedy in that predicament, and so it seemed that war would break out at any time. It looked imminent, or at least an attack looked imminent.

Well, I was not thinking about Cuba then. I thought: If, unfortunately, this war breaks out, we are going to be wiped off the map. At that moment, I was concerned about others, about the rest of the world and the Soviet Union. I was worried that a mistake would be made and that, because of such a mistake, the Soviet Union would be attacked by surprise, and that is when I decided to write the letter.

It was a very delicate thing to do since I was addressing it to no less than Khrushchev, owner of the missiles [and leader of] a superpower, the country that had played such a significant role in the world war and was playing a very significant international role at that moment. Still, I decided to write that letter.

Since I knew this subject would come up, I brought some material with me. And, indeed, this letter is dated October 26, 1962. We were in the Soviet embassy that night; I drew it up with a little pencil at full speed, bam, bam, crossing out and adding bits; I was dictating it to the ambassador. The fact of the matter is that we had given the order to shoot at low-flights by morning on October 27 and we had informed the Soviets. So, I told Khrushchev about the situation and that an attack could take place.

In fact, we were almost at war, because if we were going to prevent the low-flights, then by the morning of October 27, the antiaircraft weapons would be shooting — not the rockets, which we did not have under our command, but the artillery, all the conventional antiaircraft weaponry with a maximum range of 12 kilometers but suitable for shooting against low-flights — as we believed the low-flights were unacceptable.

It was expected then that combat could begin the following morning, not the nuclear combat but our combat against the low-flights, based on our idea that an attack on the bases could begin within the next 24 to 72 hours. This analysis was based on all the press dispatches, the information on the concentration of forces and all the debate that was taking place within the United States. We drew the conclusion that an air strike was imminent — an air attack, mind you.

I wrote to Khrushchev: "From our analysis of the situation and the reports in our possession, I consider that an aggression is imminent within the next 24 to 72 hours." I then told him of other things such as our firm stance, our determination and so forth.

I continued: "There are two possible alternatives: the first and most likely is that there will be an air strike against certain targets with the limited goal of destroying them... The second, less probable alternative, although possible, is an invasion.

"I understand that this [second] alternative would call for a large number of [their] forces and it is also the most repulsive form of aggression, which might restrain them." In other words, although I said that two things might happen, either the air raid or the invasion, I considered the invasion less likely because it was too direct, something that called for lots of forces and was much more reprehensible. An air raid might last a few minutes and an invasion was definitely a more serious event, it would have been an act of war against the Cuban Army and people, and against the Soviet forces stationed here. That was the alternative I considered less probable.

In any case, I told him what I thought: "If the second alternative is enforced and the imperialists" — this was a very common word in the language of the time — "invade Cuba with the purpose of occupying it… well, the Soviet Union must never allow the situation to arise in which the imperialists could launch a first nuclear strike against it."

I said it like that, using that phrase, because I was absolutely convinced that if they decided to land in Cuba, and once the battle had begun with the presence and possibly the use of nuclear weapons, the second step for the United States would have been a direct nuclear strike against the Soviet Union. I had reached that conclusion, and told him so as delicately as I could. Mark my words when I said that: "…never allow the situation to arise in which the imperialists could launch a first nuclear strike against it," because I was certain that the one thing would follow the other. I was explaining a logical rational.

I dictated the letter to the ambassador; took out this, put in that, underlined bits, redrafted a paragraph. I have reconstructed it from the notes I drew up, but I had dictated it to him. The ambassador did not speak Spanish very well, and there was no interpreter, so who knows what the ambassador sent. But, apparently, something of this phrase, so carefully drafted, made it through. What I wanted to say was very clear; here is the full text of the letter I dictated. This letter is opened for international opinion to see, exactly as it was written then.

I sent this letter the night of October 26, in the early hours of morning. On the morning of October 27, when the [U.S.] planes approached, our artillery opened fire against all the planes flying at low-altitude, and they actually withdrew, because a plane cannot fly at 100 meters against a number of antiaircraft artillery pieces. At dawn, our artillery people carried out their orders, so to all effects, fighting had begun. You could say that war had begun.

It was in these circumstances that, when a U-2 [spy-plane] was over-flying Oriente Province at very high altitude, a Soviet chief of antiaircraft rockets — perhaps because he identified himself with us or because he saw our artillery shoot, for whatever reason — fired a ground-to-air rocket and downed a U-2. The U-2 was shot down on October 27.

On approximately October 25 or 26, Khrushchev, through his channels with the Americans, was already discussing the U.S. missiles in Turkey, but we knew nothing about that.

He sent me a letter on October 28, saying that the message he had sent to Kennedy on October 27 "allows the matter to be sorted out in your favor, to defend Cuba from the invasion."

I responded that we had issued a five point declaration we considered indispensable for a truly honorable solution to the problem. Those five points included an end to the economic blockade, the return of the U.S. naval base territory in Guantánamo, the end of the dirty war, the pirate attacks and other similar actions against Cuba. Five correct, righteous and acceptable points.

We said to ourselves: Well, if they had already decided to withdraw the missiles they should have at least accepted these five points.

He wrote to me later, on October 30, and in that letter he was sort of trying to get back at me for my letter of October 26. It has three pages, but I will not read more than one short paragraph:

"In your cable of October 27, you proposed that we be first to launch a nuclear strike against enemy territory. You, of course, realize where that would have led. Rather than a simple strike it would have been the start of a thermonuclear world war.

"Dear Comrade Fidel Castro, I consider this proposal of yours incorrect, although I understand your motivation."

Before, we had been discussing other things, different topics. I had told him about the decision he had made without consultation, to which that letter referred, but he was talking about my famous message as to how he had interpreted it. Who are we going to blame? The ambassador for his poor Spanish? Essentially, he was referring to a message in which I had advised him that, if in fact an invasion took place, he should not allow the possibility of a nuclear strike being delivered against his country, while taking it for granted that by then we would have been wiped from the planet.

Mr. President, what a tremendous responsibility you were given at that time! What a great responsibility you had!

Yes, I believe that presence of mind was necessary. I would say that moral strength was required to dare to say what I said to him, but that was my perception. Perhaps all this would be easier to understand if I read some paragraphs from this key letter on the matter which I wrote on October 31, making some clarifications. I wrote to Khrushchev: "You yourself have said that under current conditions such a war would inevitably have escalated into a thermonuclear war and quickly." He had said that many times, that a conventional war would immediately escalate into a nuclear war. I then added: "I understand that once the aggression is unleashed, the aggressor should not also be given the privilege of deciding when to use the nuclear weapon. The destructive power of this weapon and the speed of its delivery are so great that the aggressor would have a considerable initial advantage.

"I did not suggest to you, Comrade Khrushchev, that the Soviet Union should be the aggressor, because that would be more than incorrect — it would be immoral and contemptible for me to do so. Rather, I suggested that following the imperialists' attack on Cuba and, in Cuba, on the armed forces of the Soviet Union (destined to help in our defense in case of a foreign aggression, turning the imperialists into aggressors against both Cuba and the Soviet Union), they should then be faced with an annihilating strike.

"I did not suggest to you, Comrade Khrushchev, that in the midst of this crisis the Soviet Union should attack" — I repeated this to him — "which is what your letter seems to indicate, but rather that, after the attack" — I am referring to an invasion not an air attack — "the Soviet Union act without hesitation and never make the mistake of allowing the situation to arise in which the enemy would deliver the first nuclear strike on it. And, in that sense, Comrade Khrushchev, I sustain my point of view" — I was writing this on October 31 — "because I understand it to be a realistic and fair assessment of a specific situation. You may be able to convince me that I am wrong, but you cannot tell me that I am wrong without convincing me.

"Furthermore, it was not a troublemaker who was talking to you but a combatant in the most dangerous trench.

"We knew — you should not assume we ignored it — that in case of a thermonuclear war we would have been exterminated, as you intimate in your letter. That did not, however, prompt us to ask you to withdraw the missiles or to yield. Do you by any chance believe we wanted war? But how could war have been avoided if there had been an invasion? The fact is that this event was possible, that imperialism was obstructing every solution and that its demands were, from our point of view, unacceptable to the Soviet Union and Cuba."

I had explained to him that we were well aware, if the invasion took place, that war would break out and we had already accepted our annihilation. But as a friend, I said: "If that happens, well, you have to act accordingly and not make the mistake of allowing…" because I was sure, as I am sure today, that after the invasion, a nuclear strike against the Soviet Union would have followed.

The United States has never renounced the possibility of

being the first to use nuclear weapons; it held to that idea during all the Cold War years and it still holds to it today. The United States has never renounced that position...

October 27 was a very critical day because the artillery fired [on the low-flying planes] and then a U-2 plane was shot down. But, by then, Khrushchev had already come to the agreement [with Kennedy].

I have a letter here, so you can see what Khrushchev's attitude was when the crisis broke out on October 22. It was in no way that of a cowardly man. I received this on October 23.

He spoke after Kennedy had made his declaration on the blockade. He said: "We view this declaration by the U.S. Administration and Kennedy's statement on October 22 as an uncommon interference in the affairs of the Republic of Cuba, a violation of the standards of international law and the elementary principles governing relations amongst states as well as a brazen act of provocation against the Soviet Union.

"The Republic of Cuba has every right, like any other sovereign state, to defend its country and choose its allies as it sees fit. We reject the shameless demands by the U.S. Government to control the sending of weapons to Cuba and its ambition to determine the type of weapons that the Republic of Cuba may have.

"The U.S. Government knows perfectly well that no sovereign state will permit interference in its relations with other states or will give any account of the measures taken to strengthen such a country's defenses.

"Responding to Kennedy's statement, the Soviet Government makes a declaration, protesting most emphatically the U.S.

Government's piratical actions and qualifies these actions as perfidious and aggressive... and it declares its decision to actively strive against such actions... We have instructed our representative at the Security Council to the effect that this be urgently raised before the council...

"Given the present situation, instructions have been sent to the Soviet military representatives in Cuba on the need to adopt suitable measures and to be completely ready."

Mr. President, at the same time as you were writing Nikita Khrushchev letters of encouragement, Khrushchev was in negotiations with President Kennedy over the withdrawal of the missiles. When did you discover these plans and what were your feelings in that respect?

On October 28, when one of the communications I showed here was sent, he said that he had sent a message to Kennedy on October 27 which was the basis for the solution, and which actually dealt with the withdrawal of the missiles in exchange for a hypothetical guarantee that the United States would not invade Cuba.

But there had been discussions before that — I think Bobby Kennedy had been in discussions with Ambassador Dobrynin or someone else — about the missiles in Turkey, which was even worse, because they were negotiating the security of Cuba in exchange for the security of both superpowers. It was a missile for a missile, something that had nothing to do with the signed agreement, or with principles. They were trading the missiles here for the missiles there.

It did not enter my head that such a thing could be done. There could have been other solutions. I was not proposing them because we were not negotiating with the United States and the United States would not negotiate with us. Perhaps we could have helped find a solution, but we believed it to be our duty to remain firm, to be consistent. It seems that the first agreement was the withdrawal of the secret missiles in Turkey in exchange for the withdrawal of the missiles secretly brought here by the Soviets, even though it had been their decision to bring them in secretly, not ours.

At a given moment, Khrushchev was told that Kennedy would find it impossible to accept that kind of arrangement. That is when Khrushchev sent his last message asking for a guarantee that they would not invade Cuba — a guarantee that was not even committed to in writing, it was verbal — in which case the missiles would be withdrawn.

We were really angry at this.

How did we learn of it? On the morning of October 28, the radio was broadcasting the news that there was an agreement, and that the agreement consisted of withdrawing the [Soviet] missiles and Kennedy giving a guarantee to Khrushchev. It was a disgraceful agreement.

I think that, since Khrushchev was ready to withdraw the missiles, he could have reached a more honorable agreement, suffice it to add: satisfactory guarantees for Cuba. One line: "In exchange for satisfactory guarantees for Cuba." Just adding a few words to the message. Nobody would have accepted a world war over an economic blockade or a naval base in Cuban territory. If he had been willing to withdraw the missiles in exchange for guarantees that were satisfactory for Cuba, there could have been an honorable solution. He need never have talked about withdrawing missiles from Turkey and Cuba, because that had nothing to do with Cuba's security, and then we would have again raised these demands I mentioned: Cessation of the economic blockade, return of the Cuban territory occupied by the United States, etc., almost the same demands we have now, which will have to be accepted one day. I do not know if it will be in 50 or 100 years from now but they will have to be accepted one day.

He could have added: "Cuba must be consulted." It would have even been smarter to bring Cuba into the discussions. If they had said: "Acceptable guarantees for Cuba," then we would have had to give our opinion and we would have said: "Agreed, guarantees." What are acceptable guarantees for Cuba? This, this, this, this and this, the five points we had presented that same day in the morning.

That could have been obtained and it would have been an honorable solution for Kennedy and even for the Soviet Union. It would still have been a victory for Kennedy, because the missiles would have been withdrawn without a war. But it would have been honorable for the Soviet Union in respect of international opinion and the people of Cuba. It would also have been smart to have brought Cuba into the discussions, because it would have added a small headache for the U.S. leaders — not because we had intended to be obstructive but because we would have raised fair interests.

We would have accepted and we would have cooperated. But what happened? Khrushchev accepted the inspection of the missiles here. We said: "There will be no inspection of missiles," we didn't accept it, and there was no inspection here. They were inspected out on the high seas. They had to lift off the cover of a container so that the withdrawal of the missiles could be confirmed.

Later, the Soviet Union did other things and made further concessions: they took away the IL-28 bombers, which wasn't part of the agreement. We were irritated and this problem actually created tensions and had an adverse effect on relations between the Soviet Union and Cuba for many years.

You can see how candid and forthright we were with Khrushchev, despite the fact that, at that time, we were threatened and economically blockaded. In the midst of constant U.S. hostility and threats, the material life of this country depended on the Soviet Union for fuel and raw materials. But we weren't opportunist, we weren't disloyal, we didn't surrender, we didn't waiver. We stayed firm and accepted all the risks of what was happening.

It was Khrushchev's fault that the crisis developed as it did. If he had had the common sense to do as we suggested and operate publicly, then the position of the Soviet Union before international opinion would have been very strong.

For us, it was clear that Kennedy believed the messages sent by Khrushchev; it is indisputable that he believed them, because it was the only thing he could do. It turned out that it wasn't as he was told, that there were strategic missiles here, so Kennedy was able to prove that he had been deceived.

Could you go back to the matter of the revelations from the CIA documentation? When you mentioned this matter before, when you said that Khrushchev had proof that there was a plan to invade Cuba on the part of the United States, wasn't this action — Khrushchev's decision to withdraw the missiles — less honorable, less creditable?

Well, the document I referred to wasn't the CIA's. I mentioned the CIA document with regard to the Bay of Pigs invasion, a document that has just been published and which is a report kept secret for 37 years. There was one copy left and the CIA has now released it.

The documents I was referring to are the Pentagon's, which were declassified just recently. These Pentagon papers explain their instructions in those months prior to the Soviet-Cuban agreement, on fabricating a pretext, an incident that would justify an invasion. It could have been a self-sabotaged U.S. ship exploding in Guantánamo Bay; a passenger plane leaving Cuba for the United States shot down and Cuba blamed for it; or a host of terrorist attacks in U.S. territory of which Cuba would be accused; or if the launching of the U.S. astronaut into outer space failed, to accuse Cuba of radio interference with the operation. It's possible that the Soviets had learned of the plans through espionage. You know there has been spying on both sides, that you have recruited high ranking Soviet officers and the Soviets have recruited senior officers and even people inside the CIA.

When I saw those documents, I meditated and wondered — remembering the Soviet's certainty on the possibility of an invasion — if it could be the case that they knew of those papers with the instructions for the Pentagon. They were experts in seeking information, that much we know, and they had sought information on the development of nuclear weapons at the end of World War II.

Now, Khrushchev would be able to say that he was not disloyal in the sense that Kennedy had given him guarantees. He might say that Kennedy's guarantees had removed the danger of an invasion. Do you see what I mean? But that was a very relative guarantee, and heavily debated for a long time, because we didn't accept the inspection clauses. We really didn't accept that solution.

Were Soviet-Cuban relations affected after the withdrawal of the missiles?

Yes, for a long time, for years. It wasn't public, and it did not have an impact on economic or commercial relations. They never took any kind of economic reprisal against us. They put up with our criticisms, our protests, including some public protests, they put up with them with a lot of patience. They were patient, up to the moment when we said: Who stands to gain by this? What do we get from this continuous resentment between Cubans and Soviets? What do we gain by taking this tension in our relations up to the point of a crisis?

After many years had passed and there was no invasion, we had to accept that, although the formula was incorrect and we should have been consulted, and although a mountain of mistakes were made, Khrushchev could indeed have said: "I was right, a war was thwarted and there was no invasion of Cuba." But we could equally have said that our people's efforts and capacity to struggle, its firmness and determination to defend the country from an invasion, played a significant and decisive role. Because the United States knew Cuba better, it wasn't going to make the same mistake again as at the Bay of Pigs when it was thought that a revolt would take place here. The United States became convinced that to invade Cuba it would have to pay a dear price it could not afford. Very soon afterwards, it got involved in Vietnam and in Vietnam it obtained the experience of a war of intervention against a country without sophisticated weaponry, but which was capable of defending itself with very modest military resources, by using methods of popular and irregular warfare.

Vietnam was an important experience for the United States; it could have learned that lesson earlier in Cuba, if it had invaded our country. The Soviets would not have been able to do anything.

Kennedy soon died and then came Johnson and then other presidents like Nixon and Reagan, and so many others that followed. If it had occurred to any of them to launch an invasion of Cuba, the Soviets would not have been able to do anything. If Kennedy or Johnson or any of those who followed had not honored the verbal promise of not invading Cuba, the Soviets would have done absolutely nothing because they were not willing to take the risk of a nuclear war to defend Cuba. We knew that, we were absolutely convinced of that.

The defense of our country would simply be our people's task. It would be a hard and costly struggle but we already had millions of organized, trained and armed men and women. The entire people were prepared for a long, endless resistance, that would have ended only with a complete enemy withdrawal.

We had created the subjective conditions in the Cuban population for that struggle, but if Kennedy's verbal guarantees had not been respected, nothing would have happened; a big public scandal, Cuba invaded, but no war of any kind between the United States and the Soviet Union over Cuba.

Could we go on to the 1960s?

We're already in the 1960s.

I'd like to talk to you about the Brezhnev period of government, at the time when the Soviet Union was going through a period of détente. Did it worry you at that moment that your sustained or continued support for revolutionary armed movements in Latin America could increase the tensions of the Cold War?

Well, the problem is that we were under tremendous pressure: a blockade, an economic war and permanent subversive activity within the country. After the Missile Crisis, plans continued to be hatched and implemented against Cuba: pirate attacks from bases in Central America, every kind of sabotage act, even the introduction of plant pests — that is, biological warfare against our country. In other words, the United States subjected us to a real war aimed at suffocating our country. The existence of the socialist bloc and the Soviet Union was important from an economic point of view to support our resistance and solve many of the country's problems, and we really had reached a point of mutually beneficial trade with them.

Contrary to what some people believe — that Cuban revolutionary activity was coordinated with the Soviets — it was precisely the opposite. Our assistance to the revolutionary movements was a constant source of disagreement with the Soviets. The truth is, the Soviets cannot be blamed for the activities we carried out on our own. Actually, they didn't support those revolutionary movements. In Latin America they supported none, it was Cuba acting alone.

In Angola and other African countries, the former Portuguese colonies, we had been helping the liberation movements. The Soviets were also generally helping the liberation movements in Africa. There was no disagreement over that. Different countries helped, even Western countries were helping Angola, Mozambique and others in the struggle against Portuguese colonialism. But when our troops were sent to Angola the Soviets knew absolutely nothing.

If Angola was going to be saved, ours was an unavoidable decision. For many, many years we had had relations with [Popular Movement for the Liberation of Angola leader Agostinho] Neto and with the Angolan independence movement, which, after the revolution in Portugal, was close to attaining that country's independence. Then it was invaded by South African troops from the south and by [Zairean president] Mobutu's troops from the north; both allies of the United States.

Proof of that government's association with the apartheid

regime is that while the U.S. Administration knew South Africa had seven nuclear warheads, at the time when the Cuban and Angolan troops were waging decisive battles against the South African racists in Cuito Cuanavale and in proximity of the Namibian border, they never said a word.

When Cuba made the decision to send combat units to Angola, not only were the Soviets not consulted but they were not even informed. When there were already several Cuban units fighting in Angola, helping to repel Mobutu's troops just a few kilometers out of Luanda and stopping the advance of South Africans forces which were closing in on the capital from the south, it was only then that the Soviets actually learned about the Cuban troops we had sent to Angola. They were neither consulted nor informed.

The situation was different in the case of Ethiopia. Perhaps that was the only operation undertaken by Soviets and Cubans in full agreement. Two years before, when we decided to help save Angola's independence and revolution, informing or consulting the Soviets would have created problems; we knew them well, they would undoubtedly have opposed it and serious contradictions would have emerged between our two countries.

On the other hand, we could not allow the occupation of Angola by South Africa and Zaire. Further, there were hundreds of Cuban advisers in Angola who were training the Angolan fighters when the invasion took place, so those comrades had to be saved; we could not simply leave them on their own. In old Brittania planes, over 20 years old and lacking in spare parts, we sent paratroop units with antitank weaponry, and together with the Angolan patriots they repelled the Zairean troops in the vicinity of Luanda, thus preventing the fall of the capital and halting the South Africans, who were later ejected.

To expel the invaders, at such a distant place from our country, a steady stream of Cuban soldiers was sent, with weapons, in our merchant ships. There was even a violation on our part of the agreements we had with the Soviets on arms supplies. The weapons they had supplied to Cuba could not be sent to other countries but, at that critical moment, we found ourselves forced to bypass the requirement. We sent the men and women with the weapons. That's how it was. Of course, the victory achieved gave great authority to Cuba in the Soviets' eyes.

Later, at the time of the Ethiopian Revolution, the Cubans became advocates for the Ethiopians with the Soviets, because we already had close relations with the Ethiopians who were implementing a radical revolutionary program. We supported and defended them with the Soviets, to whom we explained the importance of Ethiopia and the significance of the Ethiopian Revolution, and we convinced them to provide some assistance.

Thus, in a moment of crisis, when Siad Barre from Somalia invaded and occupied the Ogaden, putting Ethiopia in mortal danger and on the brink of total disintegration, the Soviets and ourselves undertook a coordinated action. They were also convinced that Ethiopia, an important country at risk from foreign aggression and dismantling, had to be saved.

That's the only operation where Soviets and Cubans acted in full agreement. There was no coordination for any operation in Latin America or any other revolutionary operation anywhere else. They were, in fact, opposed.

In the Angolan war itself there were difficulties. We stayed in Angola for 15 years but we disagreed with some of the tactics and concepts [the Soviets] applied there; because we trained officers and troops while they advised the General Staff in the war against South Africa. In Cuito Cuanavale and in those places, there were serious mistakes and there were always reasons for disagreement.

The second time we sent a large contingent of troops [to Angola] we also did it without consulting or informing them; this was in the final stage when the problems were coming to a head, when we needed the necessary concentration of forces.

At the end of the war, in 1988, we had in Angola some 55,000 men and women whom we had transported there in our own vessels, with our resources. This was what finally solved the problem of the South African military aggression against Angola.

There were two problems that caused great damage to the world revolutionary movements.

We are convinced that objective conditions in Latin America were more mature than in Cuba to make a revolution. Not in the same way in every country, but in a large number of Latin American countries there were better objective conditions to make a revolution than for the one we had made in Cuba. If you want to talk about that, if you want to raise any question, I'm ready to answer.

*Before passing on to Latin America, let me repeat that many people
believe there was a grand Soviet-Cuban master plan, which was part
of the Cold War process, in its attempt to dominate the world. But you
reject this, don't you?*

Look, if that Soviet-Cuban master plan had really existed, we
would have won the Cold War. Unfortunately, there was no
master plan, but quite the opposite. Cuba's actions at that time
were in contradiction with Soviet interests. The Soviet Union
was not blockaded. It had commerce with the United States,
very good relations, very good trade; the two superpowers
respected each other. But Cuba, a small, blockaded, harassed
and threatened country remained steadfast here all the time.

The United States actually declared a global war against us.
It globalized the struggle against Cuba. Its economic war against
Cuba, in order to suffocate the revolution, took that war to Latin
America, Africa, Asia, everywhere. Therefore, we also globalized
the revolutionary struggle against the United States.

It was a question of globalizing our struggle in the face of the
U.S. global struggle against the Cuban Revolution and, in that,
we didn't agree with the Soviet viewpoint. So, we went forward
with our actions but there was no cooperation; on the contrary,
there were criticisms. We still had friendly relations, they
respected our country, but there was no coordination. They were
basically defending their own interests.

As to the revolutionary movements, for us it was not only
our duty but also a necessity. When we felt we had a better

understanding of the world and we had our own experience of what the world was like — the policies of exploitation and plundering, the situation in the Third World, particularly in Latin America and in Africa — then we felt it was our duty to support the revolutionary movements. But, as I was telling you, it wasn't just a moral duty, it was a crucial necessity because we had to face up to a global struggle against our country that forced us to carry out a global struggle against the United States.

It wasn't just a problem of doctrine and a moral problem, although we did believe in our principles and defended them. It was a necessity imposed on us by U.S. policy toward Cuba.

Could we speak specifically about the struggles in Latin America?

At the beginning of the 1970s, you traveled to Chile to show your support for Salvador Allende. What was your opinion, your evaluation, regarding his policy of seeking social change through the ballot box?

We were in full agreement, absolutely in agreement. At the beginning of the Cuban Revolution, with the Bay of Pigs and all those hard years, we made two declarations — the First and Second Declaration of Havana — before enormous crowds of hundreds of thousands, almost one million people, in Revolution Square. We were responding to U.S. plans against Cuba in Latin America, since it had been putting pressure and forcing all countries to sever relations with Cuba.

Despite our position that a true revolution, a deep revolution, must be made through the revolutionary taking of power — I had these ideas very clear in my mind since before graduating from university — we considered that armed struggle should not be used while a legal and constitutional framework existed to carry forward a civic and peaceful struggle. That was our idea for Latin America.

Now, remember that in Latin America there was Trujillo in the Dominican Republic; Somoza in Nicaragua; bloody and repressive military governments in El Salvador; bloody and repressive military governments in Guatemala that disappeared more than 100,000 people from 1954 till today; in Venezuela they had Pérez Jiménez; and in Argentina, there were frequent military coups. At other times, military coups were carried out in other Latin American countries, obstructing the legal channels. So it was the military regimes constantly emerging in Latin America that closed all legal avenues. Still, our proposition, set forth in the two Declarations of Havana, was that as long as legal and constitutional avenues existed for the struggle, those legal and constitutional avenues should be used. We always defended that idea and it was the idea we truly applied.

There were several countries like Uruguay, for example, where the left was very strong and there was a [working] constitution — there, the Communist Party and the left parties acted within the law.

We spoke of armed struggle where all other paths had been closed and in Chile not all the paths were closed, and there was a strong left wing. Allende was a personality, a very intelligent man, very capable and honorable and, moreover, a man of peace. He was a very good friend of the Cuban Revolution and a man of the left, really, with a socialist mindset, and we supported the political line that he pursued. He stood for election three or four times and we were in total agreement with him. We never had any disagreements with him because, despite everything, we admitted the possibility — the possibility! — that those paths could lead as far as the construction of socialism. We admitted that idea, depending on the correlation of forces they could achieve, on popular support, on the success of the social measures and on the capacity to deal with the armed forces in each of those countries, since they could pose the greatest obstacle.

I will tell you more. When I visited Chile in 1971, in nearly every province I visited I met with members of the military. It became almost standard procedure that the heads of the military in each region would invite me for dinner and sometimes I would spend almost all night talking with them. They were interested in problems like the Missile Crisis — what is of interest to you as a journalist was of interest to them as military people. They were very interested in hearing about the experiences of the Bay of Pigs invasion, everything that happened. They were interested in the experiences of our war in the Sierra Maestra. Those military men were interested in all these experiences and I spoke about them in political terms. I tried to persuade the military that under socialism they also had a role and it could be an important role, that they need not see socialism as an enemy of the military.

We have our ideas, but we are not dogmatic. That is, we thought victory was attainable by legal means and even a program to construct socialism could be undertaken and we supported Allende and helped him in this. Who knows how many hours I spent in discussions with the military, trying to help him with them!

Mr. President, can we continue talking about Chile?

What advice or guidance did you give President Allende, specifically relating to the army or the police?

Allende was a very able man and had many well-educated Chileans around him.

We fully supported his policy and, in the area of security, we provided some advice on his personal security. Some people were trained for his personal security, something in which we had some experience since we had had to defend ourselves from those who wanted us dead. That experience we passed on to him because we thought he had enemies who might try to take his life. We provided him with some advice in matters related to personal security and even some light weapons for his bodyguards.

I presented him with a rifle which was the one he had with him the day he died at La Moneda [presidential palace]. I had given him an AK rifle and he liked shooting with that weapon. He had said that he would not come out of there alive, that he would die defending the Chilean Constitution and he honored his word without hesitation.

He had a policy in relation to the military, he spoke with the military, listened to them and tried to win their support. He had no policy against the military. As far as I was concerned and for the reasons I explained to you before, while touring the country

I encouraged the military to support Allende's policy, to remain loyal to the constitution and the law and for it to have a friendly attitude toward Allende. There were leftist forces there, but also rightist forces and there were a lot of people trying to influence the course of events.

The United States also tried to influence events. The United States maintained very good relations with the military and throughout the whole period of the Allende government, while they denied Allende credits and economic cooperation, they didn't interrupt technical and economic cooperation to the army.

In Chile, there's a very strong military tradition. From the days of the wars of independence and in different stages of history, the military had developed quite a tradition. On the basis of their interest in knowing about the things that had happened in Cuba, I tried hard to persuade them that Allende's program and Allende's political ideas wouldn't lead to the destruction of Chile's armed institutions and that a socialist country also needed armed institutions, that Cuba for example needed armed institutions, and that we had very powerful armed institutions. There was no need to advise Allende on this because he knew that he had to do this work and he actually took pleasure in doing it with the military.

Sometimes we helped because even within the left sectors there were disagreements, they did not get along. The Communist Party behaved very well. It didn't put pressure on Allende. It can be said that of all the leftist parties, it was the Communist Party that behaved most calmly, most serenely, the one that demanded least from Allende in terms of measures. Other leftist forces were more demanding; they demanded more radical measures which sometimes made Allende's political and diplomatic work with the military more difficult.

On the other hand, the extreme rightists tried to influence the army. To all this was added the growing economic difficulties that the government had to face, for lack of outside resources and also because there were many needs to cover: the need for education, health, employment and economic aid.

It is worth remembering that, in the last months of the Allende's government, $100 million of meat a year was being imported and yet only a few months after the coup Chile was already exporting meat. A popular government must attend to popular needs but that requires resources, while the economic situation was deteriorating and there were shortages of products. All of this helped create a propitious climate for conspiracies against Allende. The right wing conspired — it organized strikes, demonstrations and tried to influence the army, and all this created a situation that ended in the coup d'état. But Allende needed no advice on this, he needed help and we sincerely helped him in his political line.

I can tell you an anecdote from those days. [Augusto] Pinochet was already an important chief in the army, but when I was in Chile he was still not head of the army, he was head of the troops in Santiago de Chile. There was a military parade to honor my visit and Pinochet led that military parade. He was with me during the military parade. Afterwards, a monument to Che Guevara was unveiled and Pinochet accompanied me to its place. There were lots of people, a tremendous movement, they were pushing in every direction and Pinochet was also pushed around. As we had had this contact during my visit and because of the role he played in protocol, when I left he presented me with some books. One of the books was on geopolitics — the very term geopolitics I did not like a great deal. They also gave me some history books on the 1879 war involving Peru, Bolivia and Chile and it was a constant and incessant glorification of nationalism and the idea of the invincible warrior.

In the education of the Chilean military there was a constant apology for their traditions and their military glories which helped in creating a militarist mentality. They had the formality of the Prussians. When one of those officers stood to attention and saluted, he was so rigid it was like he was about to crack. It was pure Prussian style, more than in any other Latin American army. I remembered Gustavo Lebón who talked about the psychology of the masses and the importance of forms and formalities in some institutions. Some churches also make use of formality and rituals. The military mentality and formality is very strong in the Chilean military so it wasn't an easy task for Allende, but we hoped that, in spite of everything, a social program could advance.

How did it all end? What occurred later showed that a deep revolution was only possible in the manner in which the Cuban Revolution was made. I think the coup d'état in Chile was a blow to the idea and the thinking of many leftist people who believed in the possibility of building socialism along constitutional and peaceful lines.

Later on in Uruguay, which was then a kind of Switzerland, the same thing happened, except for the fact that there was no leftist government. The fear of a leftist government led to a military coup in Uruguay as well. That is the lesson of history. However, we have met some members of the military who raised the flags of popular struggle. An example? The Peruvian Velasco Alvarado raised the flags of popular struggle and social change, assistance for the indigenous people, the peasants and the poor, and he made a far-reaching land reform. If it was the military that was carrying out social change then we supported them; we gave political support to the military when they raised the flags of justice and social change.

Another very remarkable example is that of [General Omar] Torrijos [of Panama]. Torrijos was a military man all his life and studied in military academies, but he was also a patriot and a revolutionary. When the Panamanian military movement emerged, led by Torrijos, we gave them our unqualified support despite the fact that they were the military. In other words, we did not even rule out the possibility that the military themselves, at a given moment, could channel the revolutionary struggle.

There was a moment in the history of Brazil when the military played an important role at the vanguard of the revolutionary struggle. Luis Carlos Prestes, who was later secretary of the Communist Party, was himself a military man of military origin and he waged great campaigns showing an outstanding ability in the military field, as a member of the military. So, in Brazil, there was a tradition of military people on the left.

[Francisco] Caamaño, in the Dominican Republic, was a military man who led an uprising in order to return his country to constitutional order. He was a very progressive military man who even defeated the military putschists and the reactionary army, so the people almost had power in its hands. He armed the people, one of the most difficult things to conceive of from military academy men.

What has been one of the limitations that I have found in military academy men, even when they are progressive? They consider the idea of arming the people a terrible sin, something that should not be done. Caamaño armed the people in the midst of his struggle and if it had not been for U.S. intervention, there would have been a revolution in the Dominican Republic led by the military.

What I am saying to you is proof of how far we are from dogmatism. We accepted not only the possibilities of a revolution by constitutional means but also a revolution in which the military would play a leading role. It would not have been the first time in history, although the military, unfortunately, have certain limitations. Their academic training puts some distance between them and the people, they do not mix easily.

But there are various examples — as I have indicated — of outstanding military people. I have met some outstanding military people who could have played a role in the revolutionary struggle in Latin America.

My father was a military man.

I am glad to hear that and I am glad he didn't have to make a revolution.

Could we speak about Nicaragua and also about the role played by Cuba in Nicaragua?

Yes, we can speak briefly and also discreetly.

The Sandinista movement's inception took place immediately after the triumph of the Cuban Revolution; the Cuban Revolution had a great influence on Nicaragua. The U.S. intervention there in the 1920s, at the time of [Augusto] Sandino, had left behind it a dynasty, which was Somoza's dynasty, where the sons took their fathers' place in government while conditions of extreme poverty prevailed. The victory of the Cuban Revolution therefore had a great influence on the Nicaraguan youth, and the Sandinista movement was organized. We provided support and not in a spirit of revenge because the Bay of Pigs invasion had set out from there, but rather on the basis of our revolutionary principles. Somoza had bid that expedition force farewell and asked them to take back to him some hairs from my beard, and this didn't mean they were waiting for them to fall off — Somoza couldn't wait to have his trophy.

Anyway, the Sandinistas had our help, cooperation and support throughout many years. We also strove for unity among the Sandinistas because unfortunately they were divided.

We assisted a lot in Central America. We helped the Nicaraguans, the Salvadorans and the Guatemalans, and the first thing we did was to work for unity among the different revolutionary forces because in each of these three countries, those forces were divided into four or five groups. That was the first support we gave them. We also, however, helped in the training of their cadres and personnel and, at the end, especially to

Nicaragua, we sent as many weapons as we could. That is the story. We gave them our full support then and all possible support while they were in government.

We weren't the only ones. Let me tell you, without naming any names, that other Latin American governments were our accomplices in Latin America. Somoza had become a threat to his neighbors and to other countries. He was perceived with much hatred, various Latin American governments found him disgusting and, at critical moments, those governments collaborated with us in sending the weapons needed by the Nicaraguan revolutionaries for their decisive battles. But those names I will not disclose for the time being, I'll keep them in the files for history. I simply want to tell you that we weren't the only ones, that we can't be accused of having been the only ones helping the revolutionary movement in Nicaragua.

We did want the revolution. I should also say that we thought that revolution was possible. We were absolutely convinced that revolution was possible in Latin America and it would have probably changed the course of history; you can be sure of that.

I am also aware of the social conditions of hunger and poverty in Latin America, the abuse and injustice in Latin America where, I repeat, there were better conditions than in Cuba to make a revolution like the one carried out in our country.

We can definitely say that the subjective factors were those that failed, not the objective factors, which were certainly there. Nobody could have stopped that revolution. It would have changed the course of history and, perhaps, even political thinking in the United States. I don't mean that a revolution would have been made in the United States, but that another form of coexistence and cohabitation might have developed between the United States and Latin America: coexistence, cohabitation and peace needed by a capitalist United States and the Latin American states with social systems where justice prevailed.

Just like the Vietnam War had an influence on U.S. thinking, a radical revolution in Latin America would have had an enormous influence on U.S. policies. That's how I felt then and, still today, I think it could have been possible. It's true that times have changed, the world has changed, I'm not proposing that type of recipe for these times, I'm rather saying that's the way we all felt under those circumstances and that the revolution, for which we were fighting, could have been possible.

I was saying that the subjective factors failed, but there was also another factor: the division in the international revolutionary movement. The rift between the Communist Party of the Soviet Union and the Communist Party of China did enormous and irreparable damage to the Latin American revolutionary movements, because both countries had great influence on the Latin American left. We had a lot of influence with many leftist forces — even more than the Soviet Union — but the Soviet Union had much more influence with the Communist Parties of Latin America. The Chinese also enjoyed great prestige and influence with all the leftist parties. That division caused the fragmentation of the revolutionary and leftist forces in Latin America.

So, the enemies of revolution or socialism might one day build a monument to the well-known and nefarious historic division between the communist parties of China and the Soviet Union. History might have been different if that had not been the case. However, the course of history will change again in the future. It will change, because globalization tends to expand in an accelerated fashion and such a globalized world is unsustainable under the concepts of capitalism and neoliberalization. That's what I think.

But with respect to Latin America, and what we did and how we did it, I've wanted to point out this factor which everybody seems to forget and the tremendous harm done by those divisions as well as by the failure of the subjective factors. Those were the mistakes I tried to describe for you before. That's why the first thing we did in every country was try to unite the leftist forces and this was, perhaps, the best assistance we offered to many revolutionary movements.

You can see whether a revolution in Latin America was possible or not when in a country as small as El Salvador the revolutionaries brought the government to the brink of a collapse from which it was only saved by the avalanche of weapons, planes, helicopters, military advisers and money that the United States sent to El Salvador. Otherwise, that repressive and bloody government that at the end had no other choice but to negotiate peace would not have survived. In countries as small as those of Central America, which is not Latin or South America, a victorious revolution in one of them meant triumph was close in the others. The United States had to utilize all its resources and power in order to prevent it. Just try to imagine the significance of a revolution in other countries of the enormous South America, with incomparably better geographic and demographic conditions. That would have been a lot more difficult for the United States than the Vietnam War and without any possibility or pretext to resort to its nuclear weapons, which would have been useless.

That's why I have said and have maintained — although it is the first time I am expressing this idea publicly — that the course of history could have been different because a revolution similar to that of Cuba could have taken place in the rest of Latin America.

I should pinpoint an exception, a country where we did not apply our project to promote and support the revolutionary system: that country is Mexico. It was the only country where, in reciprocity to its policy of respect for Cuba's sovereignty, we strictly abided by the principle of mutual respect and noninterference in their internal affairs.

We could be asked: "Wasn't your policy an interference in the internal affairs of other countries?" In addition to the fact that, as Latin Americans, we felt part of the same family which one day will form only one state based on common ethnic and cultural backgrounds, we were not the first to breach the legal standards that ruled relations among the balkanized fragments into which our Latin America was divided.

The United States had been able to rally all Latin American countries, except for Mexico, in the conspiracy, the blockade and the intervention in the internal affairs of Cuba and the aggressions against Cuba. To that end, it distributed Cuba's four million ton sugar quota among other countries, including many Latin American countries. It would be worth looking at the Cuban Revolution's enormous influence on the policies later pursued by the United States in this hemisphere. Kennedy's Alliance for Progress was one of them.

If Jacobo Arbenz had carried out the reform program contained in Kennedy's Alliance for Progress, he would have been overthrown even before he actually was because Kennedy ended up proposing a land reform, fiscal reforms, all sorts of reforms.

If we set our minds to the future, revolutionary socialism, Marxism, seems to be declining, doesn't it? Does Marxism have a future?

Let's call it socialism so as not to identify it with only one of the theoreticians of socialism, albeit that the most brilliant theoretician of socialism was undoubtedly Marx, and that not all of his ideas but many of them are perfectly valid today.

In Marx's times, natural resources seemed to be unlimited. Neither oil nor gas were known at that time, coal was used. For Marx, however, the planet's resources were unlimited. There was that controversy with the famous man, [Thomas Robert] Malthus, who warned against such phenomena as demographic explosions and the limitation of natural resources which were phenomena not known in Marx's days.

Marx didn't even know modern imperialism; he knew industrialization and capitalism which he studied in England and Germany. He spoke very respectfully about the United States and he often spoke about U.S. capitalism. But Marx conceived of a global world, he didn't conceive of socialism in a single country.

It can be said that Marx was one of the theoreticians of

globalization and that globalization is an irrepressible phenomenon, an unavoidable result of the development of civilization,
productive forces and technologies. Its advance cannot be
stopped.

What matters now, is to know what kind of world globalization that will be. It is a world where nation-states are disappearing, losing strength, as in Europe where they fought each
other for so many years and now they're integrating, coming
together, suppressing boundaries; nation-states will disappear
one way or another, the trend is there. Nobody can stop globalization.

But, a neoliberal globalization, a capitalist neoliberal globalization, is simply unsustainable. One day, at least some pages of
Marx's works will have to be re-examined, because he was the
first to conceive of a totally globalized economy. He didn't think
of socialism existing in only one country, that didn't enter his
mind; and he could not have thought that Russia, the most
backward country in Europe, would be the first socialist
country: the Soviet Union.

Lenin also had a globalist mentality. He studied capitalism
thoroughly: the transnational capitalist enterprises, the un-
balanced development and the relentless struggle for markets
among the big economic powers; he also conceived of a global
world and he did not think of socialism in only one country.

They expected the revolution in Germany and other developed capitalist countries. Socialism in one country, the Soviet
Union, emerged because they had no other choice, and as
revolutionaries they could not give up. Based on Marx's ideas
they tried to build socialism in a country that was industrially

very backward, something not contemplated in Marx's conceptions. Their theoretical contributions, however, cannot be overlooked.

Future scholars will have to study these two men, and they will be more studied than [Milton] Friedman, and more than Keynes who has been important, and more than Adam Smith and David Ricardo, more than all those great theoreticians of the present economy, more than many Nobel prize-winners in economics. They will be studied some day because a global world is coming into existence and a question must be answered: What will that completely globalized world be like?

If there is any similarity between Karl Marx and Pope John Paul II, any similarity, it is that Karl Marx spoke of proletarian internationalism and Pope John Paul II has spoken of the globalization of solidarity. Looking into the future, there is still a question to be answered: What kind of a global world will that be? Will a world with a global economy be sustainable under today's prevailing concepts?

Can you imagine, for instance, 1.5 billion Chinese people, each of them with a car at the front door, when they have only 100 million hectares of arable land? Or again, 1.5 billion Indian people, each with cars at their front door?

The fact is that capitalism has not only developed the productive forces and created an economic and political system which is predominant in the world today, but capitalism has also developed models of life, consumption and distribution of wealth that are unsustainable worldwide, and which have no future.

Those issues demand responses and I am sure humanity

will find them. But they are new problems and the works of Marx, Engels and Lenin are not bibles. They were antidogmatic, and, therefore, those and other ideas will have to be developed according to the new situations.

I think your answer was that socialism will survive, that it will live on.

It's just that, some day, there will have to be a socialist distribution. Let's take Latin America, about which we have talked so much — this is the region of the world where there's the worst distribution of wealth!

You mentioned Marxism and socialism, and I don't want to make comparisons but other things come to my mind now. It also seemed that Christianity would be buried in the Roman catacombs. When the Romans occupied Jerusalem and scattered the Jews and the first Christians, nobody would have bet that, one day, the ideas of Christianity would survive over Rome's pagan ideas and would spread through a large part of the world to become a religion with over one billion followers.

When the philosophers of the French Revolution, like Voltaire, Diderot and Rousseau were proclaiming their ideas, considered to be profane and even sacrilegious, nobody would have believed that, one day, these would be the prevailing ideas in the Western world. When Danton, Robespierre and all the most radical French revolutionaries, who later guillotined each other, debated in the National Assembly and changed the calendar and created the Goddess of Reason — something that

Marxism hasn't done as yet, created any deity — nobody would have thought they were laying the foundations of the Western world.

When the French Revolution was crushed and Bonaparte's empire with it, and the Restoration and the Holy Alliance followed, nobody would have believed that, one day, the ideas of that revolution would bring capitalism's economic and political system into this world. Why should we think, then, that the ideas of socialism, which are so generous, and appeal so much to solidarity and fraternity among human beings, are going to disappear? What would prevail, then? Selfishness, individualism, personal ambition? Those will not save the world. I am absolutely convinced of that. That's what I think.

It's very difficult to talk in terms of winners or losers when referring to the Cold War. But, Mr. President, in your opinion, who won the Cold War?

The United States. The United States won the Cold War. Of course, it had very good collaborators in the Soviet Union itself.

That's quite recent history and it is still somewhat early to pass judgment on the role of specific personalities. Let's put it this way: the West won the Cold War and, basically, the United States, as the leader of the West.

I don't know if there's anyone who doubts that the socialist bloc and the Soviet Union lost the Cold War. What happened with the Soviet Union — not only the demise of the socialist bloc but also of the Soviet Union itself — was something not even Hitler dreamed of. It wasn't in *Mein Kampf*. Hitler regarded the Slavs as an inferior race, good to work in the fields, and he coveted the lands of Ukraine and of European Russia, but the demise of the Soviet Union and its fragmentation into a thousand pieces without a single shot being fired? That, nobody ever dreamed of.

Generally speaking, who lost? The Third World was also a loser because during the Cold War there were two big powers, you could speak of a bipolar world where there was space for the Third World countries to move.

Even the Movement of Non-Aligned Countries, which comprised almost every Third World country, had emerged during the Cold War and it had played a role; those countries were listened to and they were the object of consideration because each of the big powers wanted to have influence on those countries. There was talk about the Third World and about measures that might help the Third World economies as well as talk about economic development aid.

When the Cold War ended there were no longer two big powers but only one superpower exercising world hegemonism. In other words, from a bipolar world we went to a unipolar world, with huge power concentrated in the hands of only one country: the United States of America.

Sovereignty is today a completely ignored principle. The principles that rule the United Nations are outmoded and it would be most convenient at this time to have a more democratic United Nations. At the least, there should be an enlarged Security Council where the different regions of the world are represented with a right to veto — because, for the time being, those with a veto power don't want to give it up — but it would be even better without any right to veto. A more powerful UN General Assembly is needed badly.

A sort of world government, or world governing institutions, are emerging but under circumstances of only one superpower's supremacy, with all the might and overwhelming pressure it puts on the rest of nations.

There are interventions all over. Unless it is a big country like China, or even Russia, or the NATO member countries, or a nuclear power, nobody can today guarantee the sovereignty of any other small, medium-sized or big country. In other words, the concept of sovereignty is disappearing even before these countries develop. It seems to me that, from the political, military and economic points of view, there is no other power that can compete with the United States.

Some are beginning to talk about a multipolar world. I think the multipolar world will be one of the stages in the future where there will be the United States on one side and Europe on the other; with Russia, if it can overcome the great obstacles ahead, managing to preserve its own integrity and if it can resume its development; China, which is quickly advancing toward development; Japan and Southeast Asia. That is, economically speaking, there can be a multipolar world. I think that's going to be an intermediate stage before the concept, or the reality, of a truly economically and politically globalized world can be realized.

I think we would have to go through that stage where strong competition is bound to develop, and you can see this already, between Europe and the United States, between the euro and the dollar, between the Japanese yen and the Chinese yuan; no one can predict when the ruble will be in a position to join the competition. But it is most logical that strong competition develops among the different world economic powers.

Presently, the United States and Europe are competing over Latin America. The United States with its Free Trade Agreement of the Americas (FTAA), trying to hegemonically occupy as much economic space in this hemisphere as it possibly can; the South Americans with their ideas of Mercosur [economic community comprising Argentina, Brazil, Paraguay and Uruguay] and the economic integration of the subcontinent; and the Europeans trying to keep up their influence and to occupy a space in Latin America.

I mean, there is no going back to that kind of military confrontation similar to what existed at a given time and which characterized the Cold War. Another tremendous struggle of a different nature is now beginning amongst regions in the field of economics, but inevitably, everybody will march toward that global world. As the tariff restrictions and trade barriers still in force are lifted they will head directly toward that world, where they will arrive sooner or later.

Well, we have seen the phenomenon of the crisis in Southeast Asia and nobody knows yet what will happen or what influence it will have in Latin America. Uncontrollable forces have been unleashed; speculation for one, with a trillion dollars moved every day in speculative operations alone.

Millions and millions of people have become speculators, anyone of you may be a speculator because you might have bought a share on the New York Stock Exchange or any of those places, and now you cannot stop calculating and thinking about the dividends and the ups-and-downs of the stock exchanges.

Many things are still to be known. We are trying to gain more knowledge about these problems, to study them more deeply, to learn. We have groups of experts working full-time on these subjects and, personally, I am making a great effort to try to understand this world of today, its development and the evolution of the unavoidable crisis.

How far will this huge balloon grow that has been inflated in the United States with share values and which has made Bill Gates the owner of a $40 billion fortune only because his shares doubled and tripled in value?

Nobody knows what will happen with this enormous balloon that the world economy has become, and that's without mentioning other complex and difficult problems like pollution, the environment, climatic changes, new diseases, AIDS and other things that create problems for many people in the world. How can these diseases be controlled? How can the problems of development be solved evenly for three quarters of the world population?

The Third World has gained nothing from this. The Third World opposed the Cold War and wanted the Cold War to end. It even dreamed that an important part of the resources being used in the arms race and for military expenses could be used for development.

It dreamed of a possible peace between the existing big powers, between the Soviet Union and the United States, but not of the disappearance of one the superpowers and the total hegemony of the other. It dreamed of a world without the Cold

War, more concerned over the almost insoluble problems of development, but it was not dreaming of this model that exists today.

The development aid that many countries used to offer and which had decreased to a minimum of 0.7 percent of GDP (a figure that a few countries like Sweden actually achieved and that others surpassed), is decreasing further in every industrialized country, to the detriment of the Third World.

Power is in the hands of the International Monetary Fund (IMF), which often doesn't know what will happen but after the fact it says that it knew but said nothing so as not to contribute to unleashing the crisis. It's also in the hands of the World Bank, both dependent on the U.S. vote or veto, while the resources that the wealthy countries contribute for the development of the Third World are actually decreasing.

There are new competitors: the former socialist countries are now competing with the Third World for financial resources. The former Soviet Union and the group of nations that resulted from its disintegration are competing with the countries of the Third World for development resources that have been desperately needed for many years. Where are the Third World's gains? They no longer have any space to move, their sovereignty is no longer assured. Nobody would remember them now if not for their raw materials, oil and different minerals that the industries of the wealthy countries require.

The social situation in those countries is awful, many people know that — you know it and we know it well — because we have been around the world like pilgrims, like missionaries, like Don Quixote; not only our soldiers have been there, but also our doctors, teachers and engineers.

We know the real situation of that world, it's there for all to see, and it is everybody's duty to think about that, delve into it. We need to do a lot of thinking.

The Pope has been thinking, and see how he is asking for social justice. All the churches are thinking, there are lots of people thinking about these problems. We are also thinking.

We have lived through the end of an epoch and we are entering a new one, and we want to deeply analyze all these issues that have dominated our attention for a large part of our lives.

When we meet again within one or two years, perhaps I will be able to speak somewhat about these issues that I have mentioned here.

Do you feel optimistic or pessimistic about the future?

A pessimist cannot be a revolutionary. The difficulties that loomed ahead of us were so very, very big that, if we had not been the world's greatest optimists, we wouldn't have gone on.

When we landed in the *Granma* [in 1956] to resume our fighting, we were 82 combatants. We had thought of waging war with 300, but we could only bring 82. Then we were scattered and later reunited with only seven armed men. At first, I was alone with two men and two rifles, mine and someone else's, the third comrade had no weapon. We had been dispersed by a surprise attack which the enemy achieved due to our inexperience. But we learned, later we did learn our lessons well.

So, you see, such a small group of armed men was able to

reunite while Batista had many and varied resources: 80,000 men with arms. But we persevered and persevered, and our hope is that the coming generations will also persevere in the struggle with the same optimism.

But we're also realists — if you're not a realist you may lose the battle, you need to be aware of the problems. In other words, you have to be optimistic but, at the same time, realistic and you must believe in human beings, despite the fact that the human being hasn't yet given much proof of being sufficiently wise. They need more wisdom, but they can get it.

When one remembers that hardly 50 years have passed since the Holocaust occurred — 50 years since the Holocaust! — in the Germany of the philosophers, the Germany of Hegel, Kant and of all the great thinkers… When one remembers that in the cultured Germany of Goethe and Beethoven such things as the Holocaust took place, in the midst of the 20th century, one must admit that 50 years ago the tail of the primates who were our ancestors had not completely fallen off.

Now we are rapidly advancing. Let's see what you can do with the mass media and how you can help to develop culture and not to destroy it, to teach history and not to ignore it; because you have this tremendous media that can create an awareness, educate masses and spread human and ethical values.

Humanity needs to be educated. It's not just about inventing more productive machines. I am an optimist who believes that humanity knows more now; and I see trends, tendencies, movements that raise the hope for a better world.

I've mentioned the Pope, but remember, things that were unthinkable some time ago are happening today. This Pope has criticized the Inquisition, the Crusades and religious wars. He has vindicated Galileo. He has said that Darwin's theories of evolution aren't incompatible with the doctrine of creation. Listen, if a pope had said that some centuries ago, he would have been burned at the stake. Human consciousness can advance today at great speed.

There are a lot of people thinking about all these problems, and I am an optimist. I think that solidarity will prevail over racism, over xenophobia, over the lust for wealth and luxuries; I believe that generosity will prevail over selfishness and individualism. We are closing in on a new era.

You Americans, being the wealthiest, have a very great contribution to make, you should set the best example.

I have hopes, and when I meet people like you I feel even more optimistic.

CHILE: THE OTHER SEPTEMBER 11
Commentaries and Reflections on the 1973 Coup in Chile
Edited by Pilar Aguilera and Ricardo Fredes

An anthology reclaiming the day of September 11 as the anniversary of General Pinochet's U.S.-backed coup against the popularly elected government of Salvador Allende. Contributors include Ariel Dorfman, Pablo Neruda, Salvador Allende, Joan and Victor Jara and and Fidel Castro.

ISBN 1-876175-50-8 *(Also available in Spanish ISBN 1-876175-72-9)*

POLITICS ON TRIAL
Five Famous Trials of the 20th Century
William Kunstler

Introduction by Michael Ratner, Karin Kunstler and Michael Smith

William Kunstler, champion of civil liberties and human rights, reflects on five examples in which ordinary citizens were targeted for the color of their skin or the views they held. Includes essays on Sacco and Vanzetti; Scopes' "Monkey Trial"; The Scottsboro Nine; the Rosenbergs; and Engel's "Education and God." The introduction assesses the new threats to civil liberties posed by the "war on terrorism."

ISBN 1-876175-49-4

ONE HUNDRED RED HOT YEARS
Big Moments of the 20th Century
Edited by Deborah Shnookal, Preface by Eduardo Galeano

"It's the adventure of making changes and changing ourselves which makes worthwhile this flicker in the history of the universe that we are, this fleeting warmth between two glaciers."

— Eduardo Galeano

ISBN 1-876175-48-6

REBEL LIVES SERIES FROM OCEAN PRESS

ALBERT EINSTEIN
Edited by Jim Green

You don't have to be Einstein... to know that he was a giant
in the world of science and physics. Yet this book takes a new,
subversive look at *Time* magazine's "Person of the Century,"
whose passionate opposition to war and racism and advocacy
of human rights put him on the FBI's files as a
socialist enemy of the state.

ISBN 1-876175-63-X

HELEN KELLER
Edited by John Davis

Poor little blind girl or dangerous radical? This book challenges
the sanitized image of Helen Keller, restoring her true history as
a militant socialist. Here are her views on women's suffrage, her
defense of the Industrial Workers of the World (IWW) and her
opposition to World War I as well as her analysis of disability
and class.

ISBN 1-876175-60-5

HAYDÉE SANTAMARÍA
Edited by Betsy Maclean

Haydée achieved notoriety by being one of two women who
participated in the armed attack that sparked the Cuban
Revolution. Later, as director of the world-renowned literary
institution, Casa de las Américas, she embraced culture as a tool
for social change and provided refuge for exiled Latin American
artists and intellectuals. With reflections by Ariel Dorfman,
Mario Benedetti, Silvio Rodríguez and Alicia Alonso et. al.

ISBN 1-876175-59-1

THE MOTORCYCLE DIARIES
Notes on a Latin American Journey
By Ernesto Che Guevara

This new, expanded edition features exclusive, unpublished photos taken by the 23-year-old Ernesto on his journey across a continent, and a tender preface by Aleida Guevara, offering an insightful perspective on her father, the man and the icon.

ISBN 1-876175-70-2

THE GREAT DEBATE ON POLITICAL ECONOMY
Che Guevara, with Ernest Mandel, Charles Bettelheim et. al.

In the post-Soviet era, what is the relevance of Marxist economics? As minister of industry in the Cuban Revolution, Che Guevara initiated a controversial debate on the economic challenges of the "transition to socialism," in which prominent Marxist economists participated.

ISBN 1-876175-54-0

CIA TARGETS FIDEL
The secret assassination report

Only recently declassified and published for the first time, this secret report was prepared for the CIA on its own plots to assassinate Fidel Castro.

ISBN 1-875284-90-7

CUBA AND THE MISSILE CRISIS
By Carlos Lechuga

For the first time Cuba's view of the most serious crisis of the Cold War is told by Carlos Lechuga, Cuban Ambassador to the United Nations in 1962.

ISBN 1-876175-34-6

OCEAN PRESS BOOKS BY FIDEL CASTRO

FIDEL CASTRO READER

The voice of one of the 20th century's most controversial political
figures — as well as one of the world's greatest orators — is
captured in this new, landmark selection of Castro's key speeches
over 40 years.

ISBN 1-876175-11-7

CAPITALISM IN CRISIS
Globalization and World Politics Today
By Fidel Castro

Cuba's leader adds his voice to the growing international chorus
against neoliberalism and globalization.

ISBN 1-876175-18-4

WAR, RACISM AND ECONOMIC INJUSTICE
The Global Ravages of Capitalism
By Fidel Castro

A tireless advocate for a more just world, Fidel Castro analyzes
the crisis of the Third World, the possibilities for sustainable
development and the future of socialism.

ISBN 1-876175-47-8

MY EARLY YEARS
By Fidel Castro

Fidel Castro reflects on his childhood, youth and student days in
an unprecedented and remarkably candid manner. Introductory
essay by Gabriel García Márquez.

ISBN 1-876175-07-9

oceanpress

e-mail info@oceanbooks.com.au
www.oceanbooks.com.au